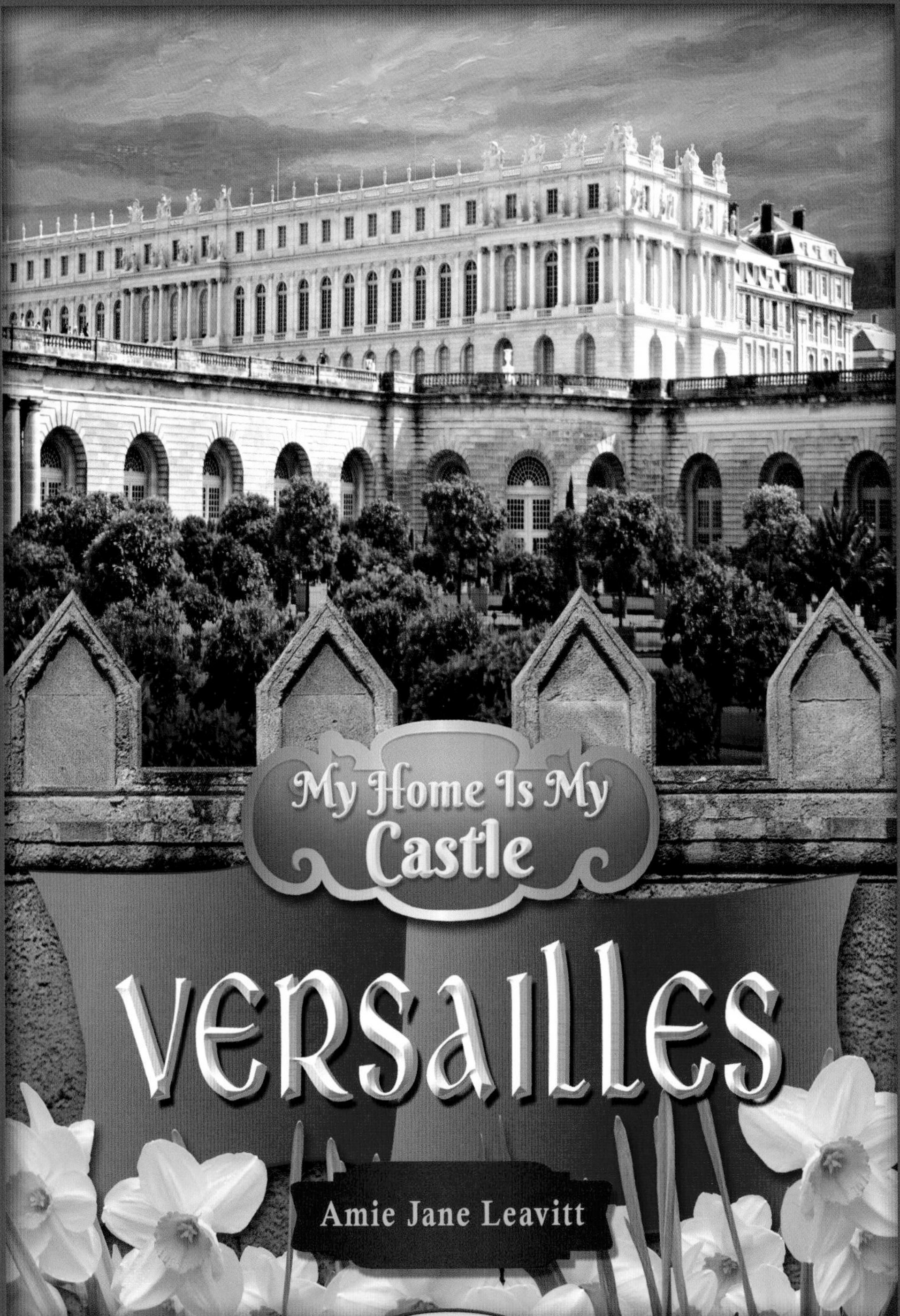

My Home Is My Castle

Versailles

Amie Jane Leavitt

PURPLE TOAD
PUBLISHING

My Home Is My Castle

BALMORAL CASTLE by Amie Jane Leavitt
GLAMIS CASTLE by Tammy Gagne
HEARST CASTLE by Ann Tatlock
VERSAILLES by Amie Jane Leavitt
WINDSOR CASTLE by Amie Jane Leavitt

PUBLISHER'S NOTE

The data in this book has been researched in depth, and to the best of our knowledge is factual. Although every measure is taken to give an accurate account, Purple Toad Publishing makes no warranty of the accuracy of the information and is not liable for damages caused by inaccuracies.

ABOUT THE AUTHOR:

About the Author: Amie Jane Leavitt is an accomplished author, researcher, and photographer. She graduated from Brigham Young University as an education major and has since taught all subjects and grade levels in both private and public schools. She is an adventurer who loves to travel the globe in search of interesting story ideas and beautiful places to capture in photos. She has written more than fifty books for kids, has contributed to online and print media, and has worked as a consultant, writer, and editor for numerous educational publishing and assessment companies. Amie has a deep love for world history. For that reason, she particularly enjoyed researching and writing this book on the Palace of Versailles. To check out a listing of Amie's current projects and published works, check out her web site at www.amiejaneleavitt.com.

Printing 1 2 3 4 5 6 7 8 9

Publisher's Cataloging-in-Publication data
Leavitt, Amie Jane.
Versailles / Amie Jane Leavitt.
p. cm.
Includes bibliographic references and index.
ISBN 9781624691409
1. Versailles (France)--Buildings, structures, etc.--Juvenile literature. 2. Louis XIV, King of France, 1638-1715—Homes and haunts—France—Versailles—Juvenile literature. I. Series: My home is my castle.
DC801 2015
914.4
Library of Congress Control Number: 2014946227

eBook ISBN: 9781624691416

contents

Introduction:
a famous alliance at versailles

On the spring day of March 20, 1778, crowds of French citizens gathered outside the gold-crested gates of the palace of Versailles. They came for one reason, and one reason only—to catch a glimpse of the famous American visitor who would be meeting with the king and his royal court today. After what seemed like hours of waiting, the coach arrived. As the guards allowed the carriage to pass through the elaborately adorned palace gates, the people cheered wildly. "Vive Franklin! (Long live Franklin!)," they shouted. The famous scientist, statesman, and delegate from America was here at the king's Chateau de Versailles at last.

Inside the gates, the official palace porters met Benjamin Franklin and his delegates. It was the porters' sole responsibility to make sure that all visitors to the palace were properly dressed. Visitors needed to wear official court clothing, crown their heads with the fashionable white wigs of the time period, and carry ceremonial swords. If visitors did not already have these things with them, the items could be rented from the palace. Though Franklin's party agreed to don themselves in the official royal attire, Franklin did not. He preferred to stay dressed in the simple style that had become his trademark in Paris; he wore a plain brown homespun suit with white shirt, white knee socks, and buckled shoes; he rested his spectacles proudly on his nose; he wore no wig on his head; and he carried a white hat under his arm. Since Franklin was so well-known in France, the porters did not force him to

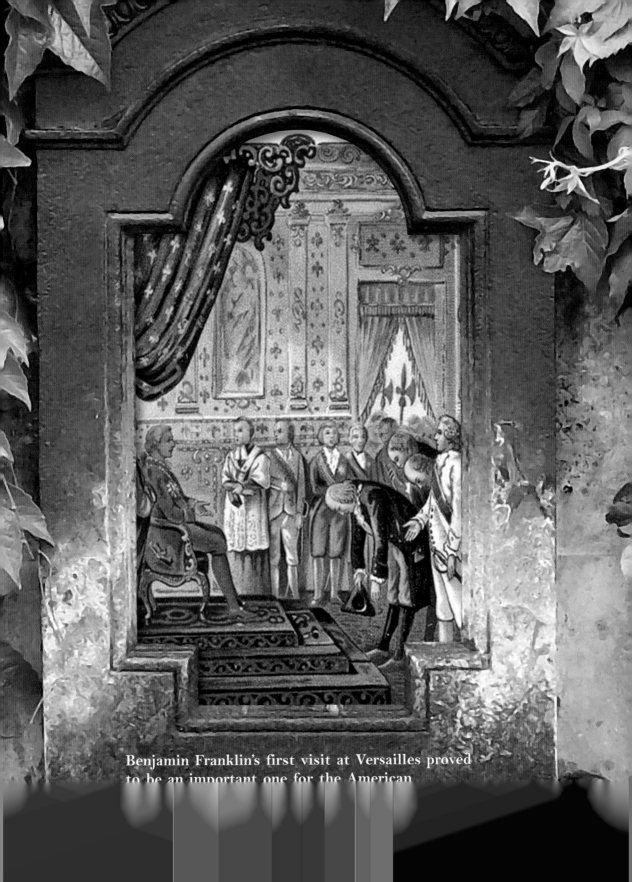

Benjamin Franklin's first visit at Versailles proved to be an important one for the American [redacted]

change. All of the nobility at Versailles dressed in clothing made from the finest fabrics decorated with layers of ribbons, jewels, and gold. They wore fashionable powdered wigs on their heads. Franklin looked plain compared to these fancily dressed aristocrats; so plain, in fact, that if the members of court hadn't known ahead of time who he was, they would have mistaken him for a common farmer.

Franklin had been in Paris since December 1776. During that time, he had established quite a reputation. He had become so famous, in fact, that the likeness of his face was now on such items as watches, rings, and medallions. Anyone who was anyone had heard of Benjamin Franklin, the famous American diplomat who was a statesman and printer and the man who had discovered the electrical powers of lightning.

Franklin wasn't in France on holiday, however. He was actually there on official business. He had been sent by the Continental Congress to represent the newly formed United States of America. France and Great Britain were bitter enemies and the Americans hoped to use that to their advantage. American leaders had sent Franklin on a mission to convince the king to side with them in the war and give them the financial and military support they needed to beat the British. On February 6, 1778, after fifteen months of negotiations, Franklin had finally secured France's aid.

On this particular day, Franklin had the opportunity to have a formal audience with King Louis XVI at his famous home at Versailles. One step inside the palace doors and it was more than clear as to why the palace was considered the most elaborate royal residence in all of Europe. Every room was spectacularly decorated with all manner of fineries—Versailles was indeed the pride of France.

Franklin and his delegates were led into the part of the palace designated as the king's private apartments. They waited in the Bull's Eye Salon, or the Chamber of L'Oeil de Boeuf, until it was their time to see the king. The room was so-named because of a special round window on one of its walls that resembled the eye of a bull.

Promptly at noon, Franklin and his men were announced into the king's private chambers. The room was in one word opulent. Every inch of it was designed and decorated to showcase the king's wealth. There were crystal chandeliers, fine tapestries, beautiful paintings, and above all, gold, gold, and more gold. There were gold-covered railings, candelabras, mantelpieces, statues, and gold-crested walls. When the delegates entered, they bowed to show respect to the king and his royal office. After the formal introductions were completed, the king gave his official approval for the alliance between America and France. He handed Franklin a letter to give to Congress. "I hope that this will be for the good of both nations," the king told Franklin.[1]

After meeting with Louis, Franklin and his delegates were treated to the luxuries that were commonplace at Versailles. They enjoyed a lavish dinner in mid-afternoon complete with courses of succulent meats, vegetables, fruits, fine pastries, and rich desserts. Then, the men were invited to participate in recreational activities at the gaming tables. It was at this time that Queen Marie-Antoinette requested that Franklin stand near her side, which was considered a great honor. The queen would generally only bestow such an honor on her highest, most important and trusted, members of the court at Versailles.

This spring day at Versailles would prove to be a monumental one for not only the Americans, but for the French as well. Change was in the air, the seeds of independence and revolution had been planted, and soon the lavish lifestyle at Versailles would be no longer.

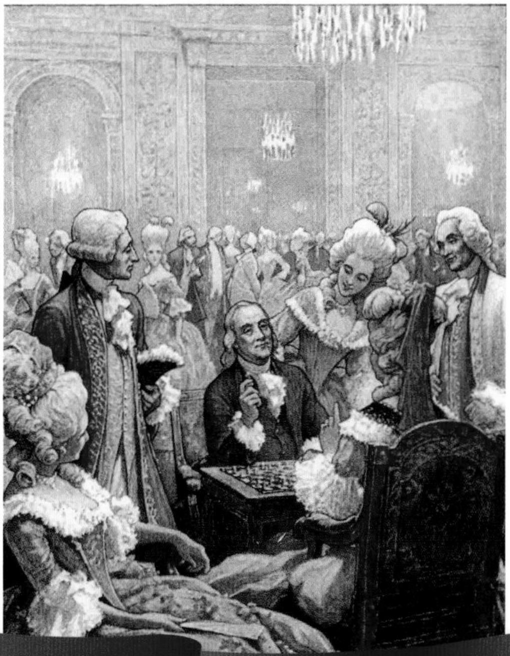

Ben Franklin enjoys life at the palace of Versailles

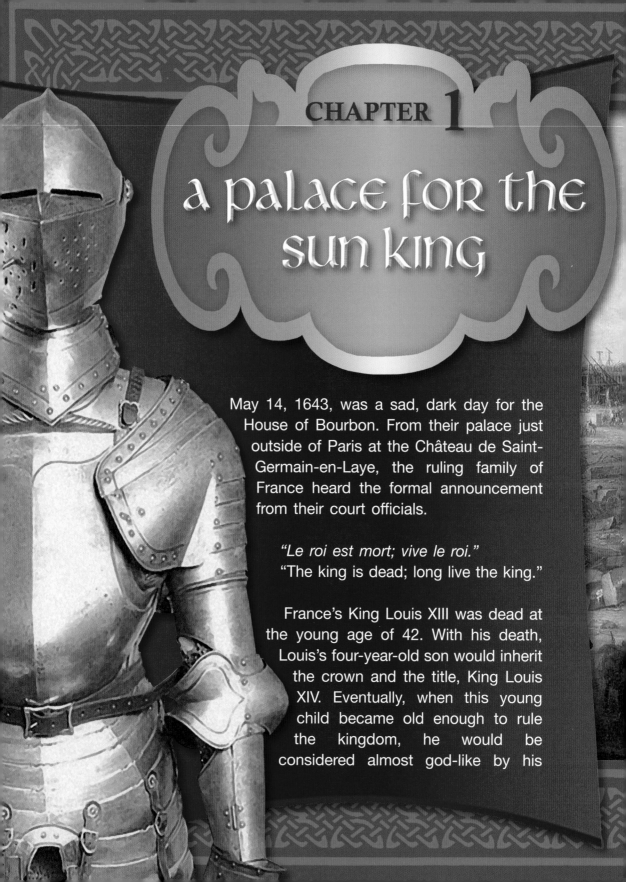

CHAPTER 1

A Palace for the Sun King

May 14, 1643, was a sad, dark day for the House of Bourbon. From their palace just outside of Paris at the Château de Saint-Germain-en-Laye, the ruling family of France heard the formal announcement from their court officials.

"Le roi est mort; vive le roi."
"The king is dead; long live the king."

France's King Louis XIII was dead at the young age of 42. With his death, Louis's four-year-old son would inherit the crown and the title, King Louis XIV. Eventually, when this young child became old enough to rule the kingdom, he would be considered almost god-like by his

Construction of the chateau of Versailles

King Louis IV

subjects. Because of that, he was given the nickname "Louis the Great" or "Louis, the Sun King."

Since Louis XIV was very young when his father died, he didn't have many memories of him. So, he wanted to make sure he preserved the parts of his father's legacy that did remain. King Louis XIII had a favorite lodge in the village of Versailles, located about eleven miles southwest of Paris, where he enjoyed spending his leisure time hunting and relaxing. Louis XIV didn't remember visiting there with his father. However, when Louis XIV was twelve years old, he went on his first hunting trip in the area and stayed at the lodge. He immediately fell in love with its surroundings. In honor of his father, Louis XIV wanted to both restore and expand the lodge and make it into a grand palace that was truly fit for the King of France. In addition to enhancing his father's legacy, Louis XIV also wanted to create a legacy of his own. At the time, kings were expected to build palaces and monuments that showcased their country's power and wealth. King Louis XIV planned to do just that with his ideas for this grand palace at Versailles.[1]

King Louis XIV chose the famous architect Louis Le Vau to design his new palace. Le Vau was a very talented architect who had designed many of the luxurious homes in Paris for the French aristocracy. He had already worked on many other projects for Louis XIV including renovating the king's other palaces in Paris. Originally, Le Vau suggested to demolish the old hunting lodge and build new, modern structures in its place. Louis XIV refused this idea, however. After all, one of the purposes of the project was to preserve the legacy of his father's favorite abode. Louis requested that new plans be drawn up that would preserve the lodge. Le Vau went back

Louis Le Vau

to the drawing board and created a model that was more suitable.

When Le Vau did so, he came up with an ingenious idea called "the envelope." He would preserve the old hunting lodge by building around it. He enclosed the old lodge on three sides with large modern structures to make it look like a palace.[2] The old lodge was still there tucked behind a facade of new brick and stone and with that, the Palace of Versailles was born.

In addition to constructing a grand palace, Louis XIV also wanted to build an elaborate garden. The original hunting lodge wasn't nearly as magnificent as what Louis XIV envisioned for his palace. He wanted to expand it to include vast outdoor spaces with ornamental lakes, fountains, flower gardens, and stately tree groves.

The only problem was that Versailles wasn't in a geographical region where these things occurred naturally. The area where the palace was being constructed was a mosquito-infested swamp. Transforming it into the paradise that Louis XIV imagined would definitely be a difficult task. France's most celebrated landscape architect, André Le Nôtre, had his work cut out for him.

One of the difficulties Le Nôtre had in designing the garden was in figuring out how to obtain the grove of trees that the king wanted. Since Louis XIV didn't want to wait years for the trees to grow from saplings or seeds, the gardeners had to find fully-grown trees in other places in France, uproot them, and transport them across France's poor network of roads to Versailles. Imagine how difficult that feat must have been. The crews did not have modern moving equipment like cranes or semi-trucks to help them accomplish their task. In the 1600s, they would have only had man and

André Le Nôtre

animal power to do such large-scale transport work. So, to aid them in their task, the men invented a horse-drawn contraption which would help them move the trees to the gardens of Versailles.

Le Nôtre designed the garden using a grid system dividing the landscape into separate geographic areas, similar to how a home is divided into separate rooms. Then, he brought in specialists to decorate each area according to specific plans. He had marble sculptures in some areas, elaborate golden fountains in others, a grand canal with gondola rides, and flowering plants, fruit trees, vegetables, and herbs interspersed throughout.[3]

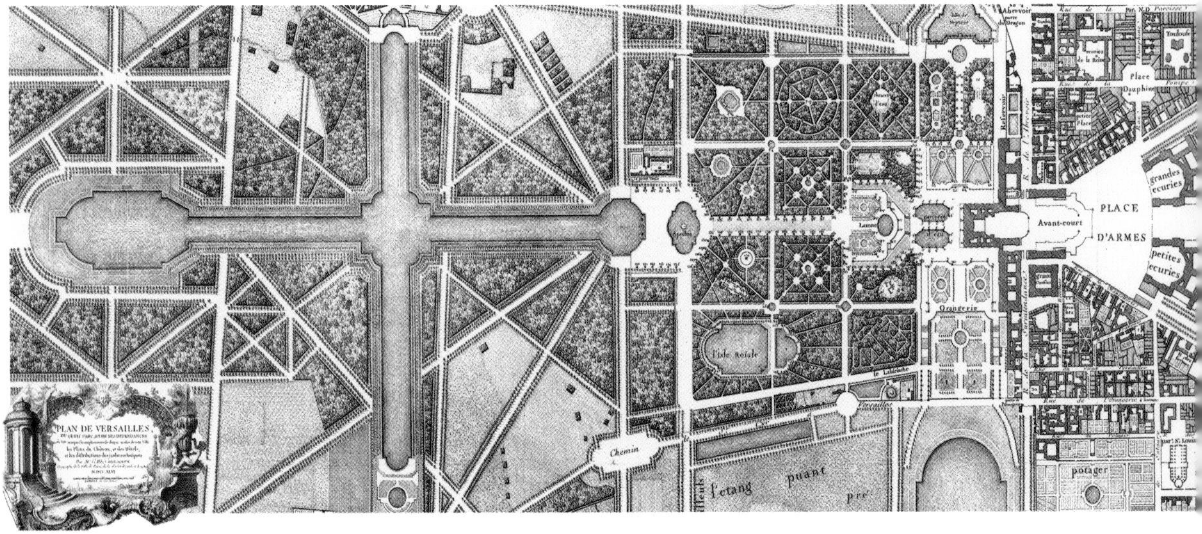

The gardens at the Palace of Versailles are still a beauty to behold, even after more than 400 years.

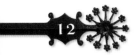

The gardens

Louis XIV loved the gardens at Versailles and was considered to be a hobby gardener himself. He helped choose many of the flowers, vegetables, and herbs that were planted there. He also oversaw the pruning and pollination of his fruit trees. He even wrote a guide book called *The Way to Present the Gardens of Versailles in 1704.* This book gave specific instructions on the best way to tour the gardens. In addition to this printed guide, Louis XIV would also sometimes lead guests and courtiers on personal guided tours.[4]

The gardens of Versailles became a favorite entertaining spot for the king. He hosted lavish parties there complete with fireworks, ballets, balls, and theatrical plays.[5] As the years went on, King Louis XIV started spending less and less time in Paris and more and more time at Versailles. Because of that, Louis XIV decided to move his entire court there to live permanently in 1677.[6] That meant that the seat of the French government would be at Versailles. To do so meant that even more construction on the palace grounds needed to take place. The king's court was massive—it included tens of thousands of courtiers, government officials, and servants. All of these people needed places to live, to engage in royal business, to relax, and to entertain at the new palace. So, the Versailles construction project just kept on getting bigger and bigger and the palace continued to grow.

Versailles is located to the southwest of Paris in the central part of France.

This construction required a vast amount of workers. At the height of the project, it is estimated that approximately 40,000 laborers worked on building the grand palace. Since Louis XIV was impatient for his palace to be completed, construction continued on the project day and night, without any regard for the safety of the workers. It was all deemed necessary for the cost of building the king's grand home. Because of the dangerous working conditions, many laborers were either seriously injured or killed while working.

When Versailles was all finished, the palace was truly a magnificent place for the king and his court to dwell. Yet, building it came with a significant price both in financial resources and in human life. It is estimated that the palace would have cost between two and three billion dollars to build today. The palace has 700 rooms, more than 2,000 windows, 67 staircases, 1,250 chimneys, and can house up to 20,000 people.[7]

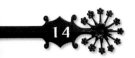

THE HALL OF MIRRORS

In 1670, Louis Le Vau had passed away and so a new architect took his place. His name was Jules Hardouin-Mansart and he had been one of Le Vau's students. It was by Mansart's designs that most of the buildings at Versailles were constructed. One of his most impressive designs was for the exquisite Hall of Mirrors, which is still considered one of the most spectacular features of the entire palace and one of the most beautiful rooms in the world.

This 240-foot-(73-meter-) long hall is 34 feet (10 meters) wide with a 40-foot (12-meter) ceiling. It is lined on one side with seventeen tall arched windows lined in gold that look out over the palace gardens. On the opposite wall, there are matching arches that hold more than 578 hand-crafted mirrors.[8] In the 1600s, mirrors were extremely expensive. In fact, even the smallest hand-mirror was considered a luxury item reserved only for the wealthy. That was because the process of making mirrors was both difficult and dangerous. Therefore, the presence of so many mirrors in one hall proved that no cost was spared when it came to building the king's palace.

The mirrors reflect the sunlight from the windows and illuminate the room. The walls of the marble hall are gilded in gold and its ceilings are painted with frescoes. In many of these ceiling paintings, the king is the central figure or hero. Dozens of candelabra chandeliers crafted out of sparkling crystal hang from the arched ceiling and gold furniture and marble statues are placed strategically throughout the long walkway.

The Hall of Mirrors has been the site of many important events throughout history. In 1919, it was the site where the Treaty of Versailles was signed which ended World War I. In 1961, French President Charles de Gaulle hosted a lavish state dinner in the Hall of Mirrors for the newly elected U.S. President John F. Kennedy and First Lady Jacqueline Kennedy.

Today, when people come to Versailles, the Hall of Mirrors is usually top on their list of rooms to visit.

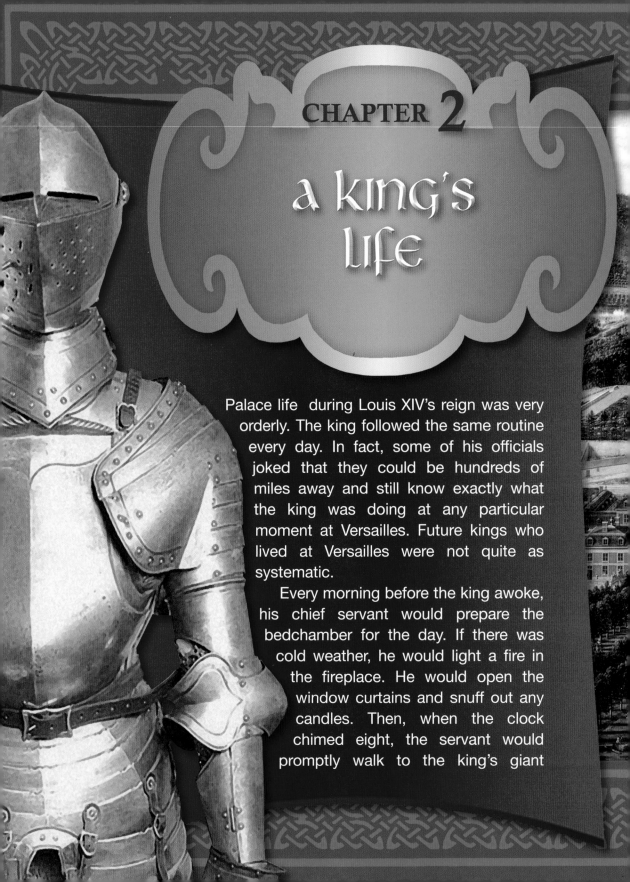

CHAPTER 2

A King's Life

Palace life during Louis XIV's reign was very orderly. The king followed the same routine every day. In fact, some of his officials joked that they could be hundreds of miles away and still know exactly what the king was doing at any particular moment at Versailles. Future kings who lived at Versailles were not quite as systematic.

Every morning before the king awoke, his chief servant would prepare the bedchamber for the day. If there was cold weather, he would light a fire in the fireplace. He would open the window curtains and snuff out any candles. Then, when the clock chimed eight, the servant would promptly walk to the king's giant

The entrance to Versailles is just as magnificent as the palace itself.

To be invited into the king's private quarters was considered a great honor.

four-poster bed, which was shrouded behind a thick red embroidered curtain, and say, "Sire, it is the hour." The king would spend a few minutes waking up and then finally allow his bed curtains to be opened. Once he did so, the royal children were permitted to come in and say good morning to their father.

Following their visit, a variety of people would come in at different times over the next two hours to observe the king as he got ready for the day. Some came in while he said his morning prayers. Others came in while his servants shaved his beard or while he chose which wig he would wear for the day. Still others came in to watch him eat his breakfast on porcelain and golden dishware. This might sound dull or uninteresting to watch someone do these mundane tasks. But during this time period, it was actually considered a great honor to be invited into the king's "levee," as these morning rituals were called. Courtiers in Louis XIV's court could only hope that they would one day be lucky enough to be invited to share these private moments with the king.

Promptly at ten o'clock, the king would make his formal procession towards his chapel for morning mass. When he left his apartments, his courtiers would line the grand Hall of Mirrors hoping to greet him, or at least have a glance at him. It was very important as a courtier to make your presence known to the king as often as possible. There was nothing more tragic for a courtier than to hear the king say about him, "I do not know him; he is a man I never see."[1] Receiving favors from the king or positions of authority in government only happened when the king actually knew a person and saw him or her often.

After the king spent thirty minutes worshiping, he returned to his apartments to meet with various councils for the rest of the morning. On some days he would meet with his council of state. On other days he would meet with his councils of finance and religion. Sometimes he would even take a tour of his building projects to inspect the works in progress. It was at all of these council meetings that important decisions were made on how the kingdom would run.

At one o'clock, the king would eat lunch, and usually he did so alone. He would sit at a table in his bedchamber and look out the windows over his magnificent gardens. Every meal at Versailles was a spectacular affair with many courses. The king's food was always brought to him under the watchful eyes of the palace guards. Before the food was presented to the king, a few select servants were required to eat a "trial" of the food and drink a "trial" of the wine. This made sure that the food and drink were safe for the king to consume and that neither was poisoned.

In the morning, the king decided what his afternoon schedule would entail. Sometimes, he spent it walking through the gardens. Other times he would go on a hunt or practice target shooting with his advisors. The woods surrounding Versailles were filled with all kinds of wild animals like foxes, roebucks, deer, wolves, rabbits, and wild boars. In addition, Louis XIV spent some time feeding and tending to his dogs. By six o'clock, the king would be back at the palace where the Dauphin, or heir to the throne, would

A royal dining room

manage the evening's entertainment. The king would spend this time in his own apartment signing letters or taking care of other business of the kingdom. Then, he would spend some quality time with his queen before dinner.[2] Louis XIV was married to Maria Theresa of Spain until she died in 1683. Then, the king was married to Madame de Maintenon until his death in 1715.

Promptly at ten o'clock, the Grand Public Supper would be served. This was a magnificent event where large crowds of courtiers were invited to join the royal family in a lavish meal. The meal would last for at least an hour and included many different courses. The first course, or service, was the appetizers. Then, came the soup course, the roasted meats course, and the salad course. The dessert course came next which was then followed by the fruit service. The courses were always brought in on plates made of pure gold, silver, or the finest porcelain.[3]

When the king was finished, he would retire to his bedchamber. Just as his morning routine was viewed by a sampling of "lucky" courtiers, so was his evening routine. While the morning routine was called the "levee" which means "to rise," the evening routine was called the "couchée" which means to "lie down or put to sleep." During this evening ritual, certain people were allowed to watch the king remove his hat, gloves, cane, and sword. Other people were allowed to come in while the king said his evening prayers. Another group of courtiers was allowed to watch the king wash his face and hands in a silver basin.

Once the king was ready for bed, everyone would leave his room. Sometimes he would take this opportunity to play with his dogs again who stayed in the adjoining room. Or sometimes he would just relax and read a book. Most of the time, though, the king would be so tired after his long day that he would close his bed's curtains and drift off to sleep. After all, he had to be up bright and early the next day at eight o'clock in the morning to begin his routine all over again.[4]

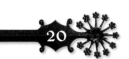

LIVING THE GOOD LIFE

Louis XIV

Versailles quickly became known as a place where elaborate celebrations and festivals occurred. These were only attended, of course, by the royal family and the nobility. The common people—which consisted of the majority of France's population—were never invited.

The first of these celebrations hosted by Louis XIV was called "The Pleasures of the Enchanted Island." It was held in May 1664. This grand festival lasted for six days and was attended by 600 guests. During that time, there were elaborate horse parades where the king took center stage and led the rest of the riders along the parade route. He wore a scarlet-red riding costume and his horse was outfitted with a gold and silver saddle that was adorned with precious jewels. In the evenings, there were ballets, theatrical performances, balls, masquerades, and operas. To conclude each day of the festivities, the attendees watched magnificent fireworks displays in the gardens that were set to the music of Vigarani.[5]

Once Louis XIV moved his court here to live permanently, the social calendar was more clearly defined. Every year, the calendar was divided into three social seasons. The first season was the winter carnival. The second season was the Easter celebrations. The third season was the summertime festivities. During the winter season, the court generally went on formal hunts every afternoon either on foot or on horseback. In the evenings during the winter season, the king held formal receptions which included balls, masquerades, concerts, and games of chance. The king always left the reception and went to bed before midnight. However, the party would sometimes continue until dawn with the courtiers dancing and feasting all night long. During the spring and summer seasons, the afternoon entertainment included boat rides on the Grand Canal, walking or carriage tours of the gardens and orangerie, and visits to the stables to watch the training of the royal horses. The evening entertainment was very similar to the winter season with elaborate masquerade balls being the most popular. Often, courtiers would change their elaborate costumes and intriguing masks two or three times in one night.

The clothing worn at these formal functions was elaborate and also very expensive. In 1714, Louis XIV invited the ambassador of Siam to a royal function at Versailles. The king wore a piece of clothing called a "habit" that was like a long cape. It was made out of black velvet fabric and was embroidered with gold and studded with diamonds. This habit would have been valued at more than 2.5 million dollars.[6]

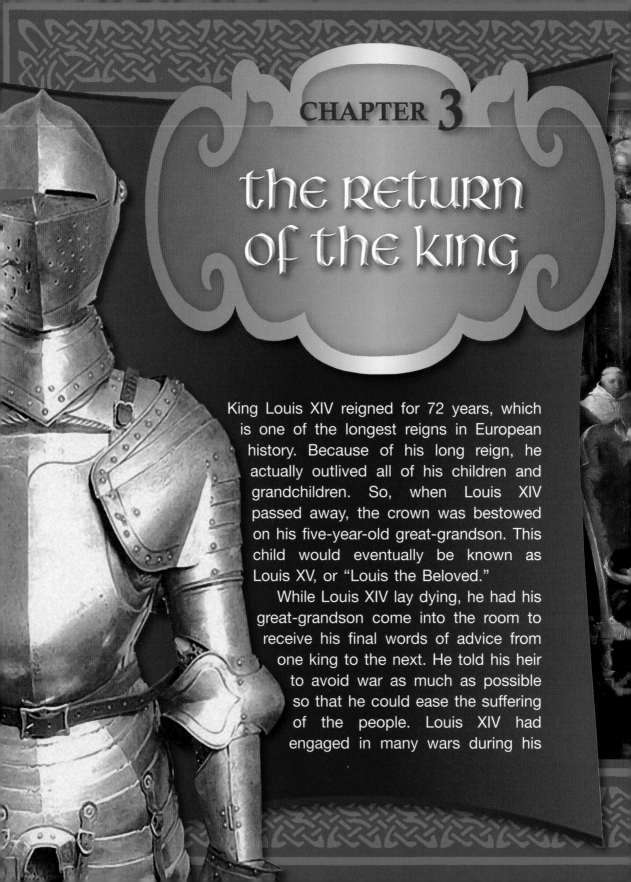

CHAPTER 3

The Return of the King

King Louis XIV reigned for 72 years, which is one of the longest reigns in European history. Because of his long reign, he actually outlived all of his children and grandchildren. So, when Louis XIV passed away, the crown was bestowed on his five-year-old great-grandson. This child would eventually be known as Louis XV, or "Louis the Beloved."

While Louis XIV lay dying, he had his great-grandson come into the room to receive his final words of advice from one king to the next. He told his heir to avoid war as much as possible so that he could ease the suffering of the people. Louis XIV had engaged in many wars during his

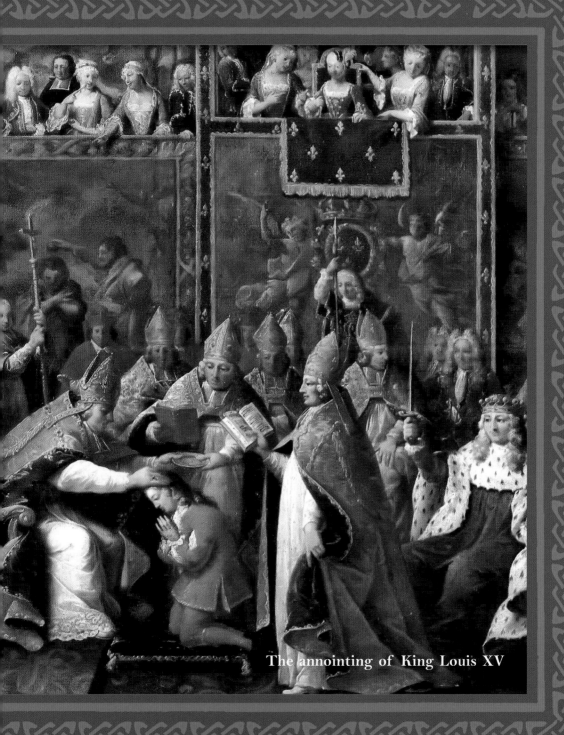

The annointing of King Louis XV

reign, and had now regretted it. He hoped his heir would not make the same mistakes that he had.

In France and other European nations with monarchies, life for a royal child was very different from the life of a common child. Louis XV had all of the luxuries that he could possibly want. He had fine clothing to wear, delicious food to eat, and beautiful gardens to romp and play in. Louis XV was raised almost entirely by a governess. Royal parents rarely had much to do with the raising of their children—they were just far too busy with matters of the court and the kingdom. However, in Louis XV's case, he was raised by a governess because his own parents had passed away when he was only two years old. As a child, Louis XV lived a rather lonely life. His only sibling, his older brother, had died of smallpox at the same time Louis's parents had passed away. He was left to grow up on his own.[1]

Louis XV was the first king of France to be born at Versailles. Yet, he would not spend the majority of his childhood there. After Louis XIV's death, the court abandoned Versailles and went back to Paris to dwell at the Tuileries Palace. However, when Louis XV was old enough to be officially crowned king at age 12, he was also old enough to make his own decisions about where he wanted to live. He decided that he wanted to return the government seat back to his great-grandfather's beloved country palace at Versailles. He was bored in Paris and longed for the luxury and wide open spaces that Versailles had to offer.

It was a delightful summer afternoon on June 15, 1722, when Louis XV returned with his entourage to Versailles. They rode down the avenue de Paris in royal chariots and the crowds from the nearby towns gathered to cheer for the return of their king. As soon as Louis entered the palace grounds, he immediately went to the king's chapel. There, he knelt at the altar and prayed. This was a symbolic gesture that showed he was a true "Christian king." Then, as any 12-year-old boy would want to do, the next stop on his agenda was the gardens. He raced out into the long expanses of lawn to explore the many areas of his great-grandfather's beloved oasis. He wandered through the famous orangerie, explored the manicured fruit orchards and groves, visited the animals in the menagerie, delighted in the

The royal family lived a very lavish life at Versailles. The hairstyles, clothing, and furnishings in this picture are indicative of their elaborate existence.

water fountains, and took gondola rides on the grand canal. He then spent many hours visiting all of the grand royal apartments in the palace. Finally, he made his way to the spectacular Hall of Mirrors—which was a perfect spot for him to end his day's exploration. As was also typical behavior for a 12-year-old boy, the king entered the room and did something that an adult would never dream of doing. He immediately lay on his back on the hardwood floor so he could get a better view of the beautiful ceiling paintings. The funniest part came next—as the young king lay there on the palace floor, he was soon joined by all of his courtiers. Here were these adult men in their regal attire, donned with expensive jewelry and powdered wigs, lying on the floor of the palace looking up at the heavenly ceiling. They likely thought that if it was okay for their king, then it was okay for them.[2]

The palace gardens include many indoor greenspaces. This particular one is called the Jardin des Serres d'Auteuil.

At Versailles, Louis XV was educated by private tutors. They taught him history, geography, science, and politics. Louis particularly loved his science lessons. He studied botany (the science of plants), medicine, and astronomy. Later in life, he funded many scientific missions. He sent mariners out to distant lands to retrieve plant specimens so he could study them at Versailles. He let scientists come into the gardens and classify the plants there. He also had a greenhouse built in the gardens. In this special building, plants from all over the world could be grown. He had more than 4,000 varieties of plants growing in this climate-controlled plant conservatory.[3] Louis XV also advanced science by funding the cartography activities of his country's engineers and geographers so that proper maps could be made of his kingdom.

CHOCOLATE AT VERSAILLES

Hot chocolate

Louis XV was known for his love of chocolate. During his time, chocolate was mainly consumed as a hot drink like "hot chocolate" is today. Years before, Louis XIV had made chocolate a very popular drink amongst the courtiers at Versailles, and Louis XV followed with that tradition. Louis XV even made his own hot chocolate in his private apartments using his own special recipe.

In 1755, Louis XV's favorite recipe for hot chocolate was published by a French cookbook author named Menon and is now on the palace's official web site.

Louis XV's Hot Chocolate Recipe

"Place the same quantity of chocolate bars and glasses of water in a coffee maker and boil gently; when you are ready to serve, place one egg yolk for four servings and stir over a gentle heat but do not boil. If prepared the night before, those who drink it every day leave a leaven for the one they make the next day; instead of an egg yolk you may use a whisked egg white after having removed the first mousse, mix it with some of the chocolate from the coffee maker then pour back into the coffee maker and finish the preparation as with the egg yolk."[4]

CHAPTER 4

A NEW AGE IS BREWING

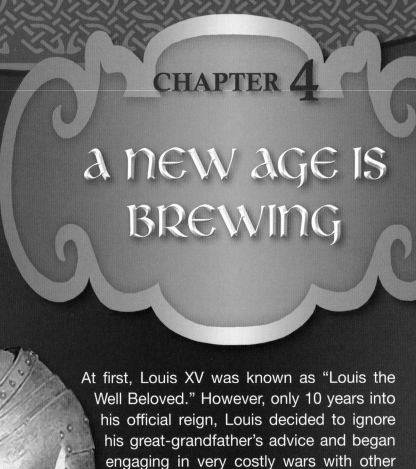

At first, Louis XV was known as "Louis the Well Beloved." However, only 10 years into his official reign, Louis decided to ignore his great-grandfather's advice and began engaging in very costly wars with other nations. There was the War of the Polish Succession in 1733, the War of the Austrian Succession in 1740, and the Seven Years War from 1756 to 1763.

These wars proved to be very expensive for the kingdom and the people of France began to struggle because of the heavy tax burden they had to pay. Not only were the wars expensive, but so were the lifestyles of the royal family and the aristocracy. It is estimated that it cost anywhere from six to twenty-five

France had planned on invading their arch-nemesis, Great Britain. However, those dreams were squashed with the costly Battle of Quiberon Bay in 1759.

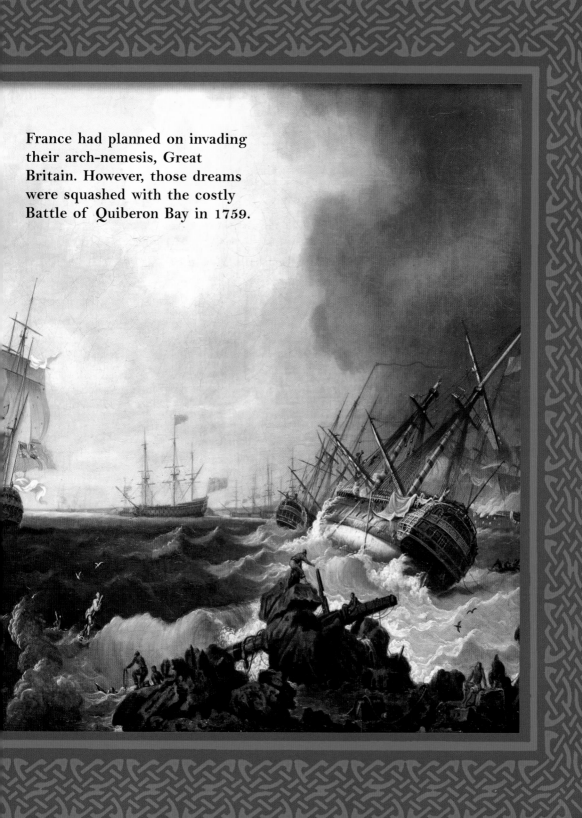

percent of the entire French government's income to pay for the general upkeep of Versailles and the many lavish parties, balls, dances, and feasts that were held there.[1] The aristocracy did not pay taxes—thus, the poor people of France were responsible for the extravagant lifestyle that the wealthy were living.

By the time Louis XV died of smallpox in 1774, very few people were upset at his passing. They were becoming more and more disenchanted with the king, the royal family, and the elaborate lifestyle of the people who lived at Versailles. Louis XV's successor, Louis XVI, would inherit a kingdom that was very much in debt and ripe for revolution. Louis XVI began his reign as king of France at the age of 20. Unlike his two predecessors before him, Louis XVI had married before becoming king. In 1770, at the age of 16, he wed Austrian princess Marie-Antoinette.

Louis XVI, Marie-Antoinette, and family in 1782

Marie-Antoinette loved to entertain. Here she plays the harp for guests.

Marie-Antoinette loved entertaining at the palace. She held lavish balls at least three times a week. She hosted other court events like theatrical plays, concerts, and operatic performances. The queen loved fashion. She had her own designer and dressmaker at the palace named Rose Bertin, who was formerly known as the Minister of Fashion.

Frequently, Marie-Antoinette liked to escape the rigors of court life at the palace and retreat to her own private abode. Her husband gave her the Petit Trianon, an estate on the outskirts of the palace grounds. Here, she had a lavish theater built in 1780. Then, she had a hamlet built in 1783.

The hamlet was a rustic country-style village complete with eleven houses that surrounded a large lake. Five of the houses were specifically used by the queen and the other four were used by the peasants who maintained the property. All of the food was prepared in a separate house (so that the queen's house wouldn't get too hot) and served on fine china. The peasants worked the land and kept the houses clean and presentable for her.[2]

French soldiers were there when General Cornwallis surrendered to George Washington at the Battle of Yorktown–the battle which ended the American Revolution.

Early on, Louis XVI was advised about the financial problems his country faced. He was instructed by his finance ministers that the only way to solve the problem was to start taxing the nobility—or rather, the people who lived with Louis at Versailles. This would not be received well by his associates at court; after all, no one would want to have part of their money taken away for taxes, especially if they never had to pay them in the past. The aristocracy believed that someone else, anyone else, was responsible for paying the national debt. As long as they didn't have to pay it, they didn't care who did.

These financial problems reached their peak in 1778. That's when Louis XVI agreed to help the Americans in their war against the British. The king was hesitant at first—while he and his countrymen detested the British, he did not want to encourage the act of revolution among his own subjects. Louis eventually decided to put those concerns aside and agreed to help the Americans. By doing so, the course of history was forever changed for both America and France.

WORLD'S FIRST HOT-AIR BALLOON FLIGHT

Balloon flight at Versailles

During Louis XVI's reign in 1783, the first aerostatic flight in the world occurred at Versailles. The scientists and inventors Joseph-Michel and Jacques-Etienne Montgolfier had been working for more than a year on their hot-air balloon project and had finally perfected it enough to showcase it for the king. The brothers had experimented with many different types of fabrics and found one that was made of cotton to be the best choice. Their balloon measured about 60 feet (19 meters) high, 44 feet (14 meters) wide, and 881 pounds (400 kilograms) in weight. That's the same height as a six-story building, the same width as a school bus, and the same weight as four baby elephants.

On September 19, the brothers prepared their balloon in the courtyard. The royal family stood out on the balcony waiting for the big moment. Promptly at one o'clock, a cannon boomed which signaled that the balloon's wicker basket was to be loaded with its precious cargo: a duck, a rooster, and a sheep. Then, at exactly 1:11P.M., another cannon boomed. It signaled that the balloon was about to rise. And sure enough, it did. The huge blue balloon rose into the sky high above the palace. The royal family and courtiers were delighted. The balloon flew for exactly eight minutes before a tear in the balloon caused it to descend. It traveled for approximately two miles (4 kilometers) at a height of 1,640 feet (500 meters). When it landed, the animals were still nestled safely inside.[3]

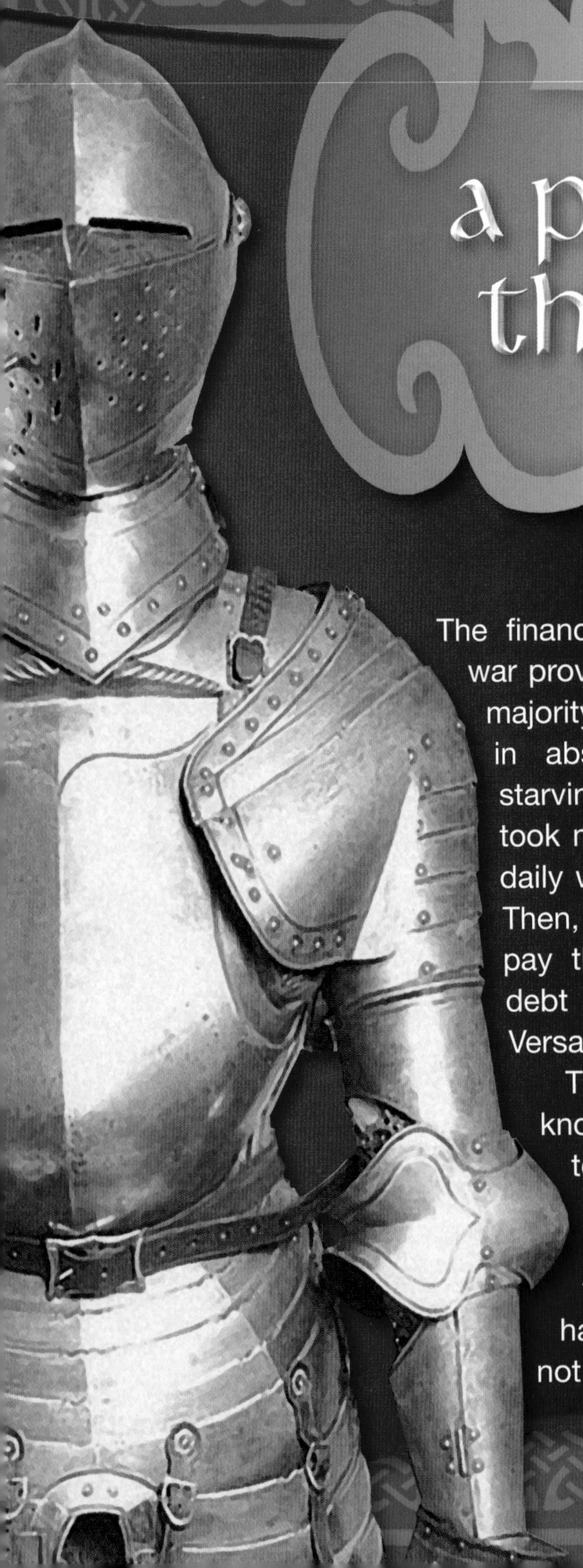

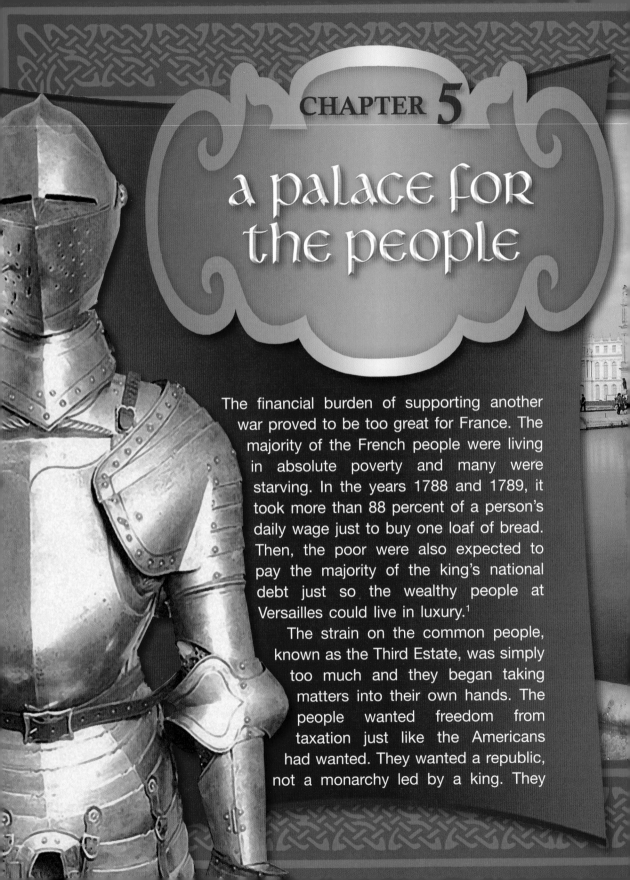

CHAPTER 5

a palace for the people

The financial burden of supporting another war proved to be too great for France. The majority of the French people were living in absolute poverty and many were starving. In the years 1788 and 1789, it took more than 88 percent of a person's daily wage just to buy one loaf of bread. Then, the poor were also expected to pay the majority of the king's national debt just so the wealthy people at Versailles could live in luxury.[1]

The strain on the common people, known as the Third Estate, was simply too much and they began taking matters into their own hands. The people wanted freedom from taxation just like the Americans had wanted. They wanted a republic, not a monarchy led by a king. They

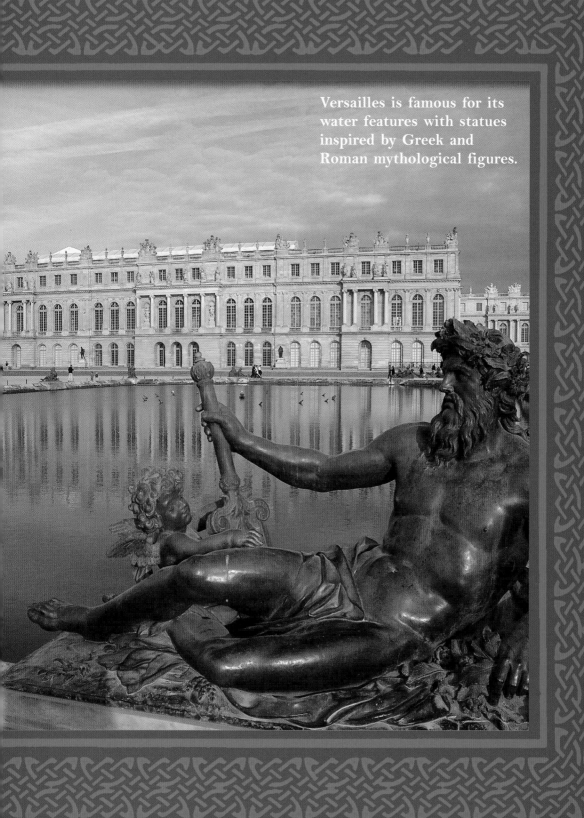

Versailles is famous for its water features with statues inspired by Greek and Roman mythological figures.

The people of the Third Estate finally had enough. They stormed the Bastille to get the weapons they needed for revolution. Eventually, they marched on Versailles and captured the "Baker, the Baker's Wife and the Baker's Son" which is how they referred to the King, Queen, and Dauphin.

formed the National Guard with their colors of red, white, and blue. Pandemonium erupted in the streets of Paris. The revolutionaries stormed the Bastille to obtain the large stores of weapons and ammunition that were stored there. The French Revolution had begun.

On October 1, 1789, everything was still progressing just as usual for the people at Versailles, as if nothing unusual was going on in the world around them. That night, the court held another of their lavish feasts for 210 guests. The royal family and courtiers sat along the expansive banquet table and ate, drank, danced, and enjoyed revelry just like they always had. But this time, it was too much. The rest of the country was starving to death and the aristocracy at Versailles clearly did not care.

Five days later, on October 6, 1789, an angry mob set out for Versailles. They broke through the golden gates and began storming through the doors. The crowd demanded that the royal family come with them to Paris. The royals who were at Versailles were outnumbered and outgunned. The king wanted to avoid civil war, so he agreed to go with the mob to Paris. He took along his family and most of the French Assembly. Little did he know that when he left Versailles on that cold, October morning that he would never return.

Once King Louis XVI and Queen Marie-Antoinette left the palace, the rest of the aristocracy went into hiding, fearing for their own lives and safety. The French Revolution was a brutal one and many people lost their lives.

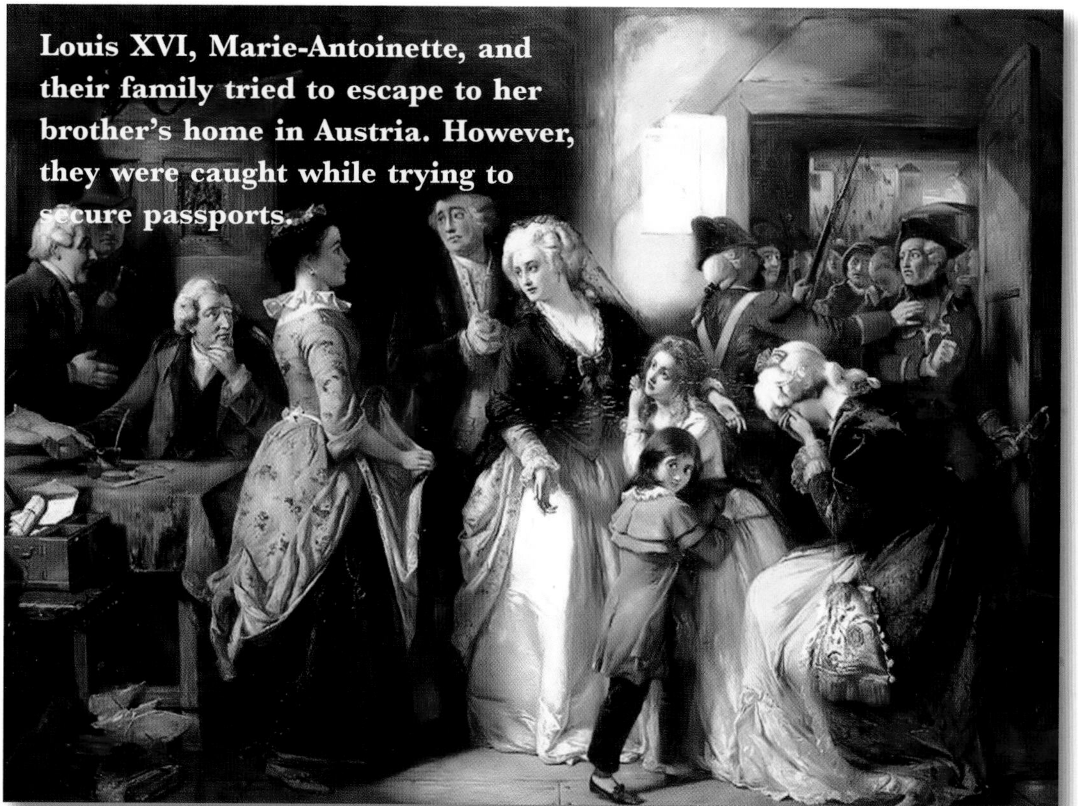

Louis XVI, Marie-Antoinette, and their family tried to escape to her brother's home in Austria. However, they were caught while trying to secure passports.

Louis XVI returns back to Paris under guard. He eventually would be taken to the guillotine.

King Louis and Marie-Antoinette met that fate. They were both executed in 1793. The French monarchy and the Bourbon Dynasty officially came to an end and the golden years at Versailles became a thing of the past.

Years later, in 1833, the Palace of Versailles was turned into a museum owned by the French and has been one ever since. Today, Versailles is one of the most famous places to visit in all of France and the 39th most popular place to visit in the entire world (according to Travel and Leisure magazine).[2] Approximately 5.9 million people visit the palace each year.

The best time to visit, if you want to avoid the crowds, is during the fall. The weather is temperate so you can still enjoy the palace gardens, and there are far fewer tourists there than during the summer months. Wintertime is also a good time to visit. But the weather can be quite cold and the gardens are often covered in snow.

Anytime is a good time to visit the palace online. On its official web site, you can read all about the history of the palace, learn about the people

The Hall of Mirrors is one of the most spectacular rooms in the world and is a treasured place to visit at Versailles.

Visitors should plan on spending at least a full day at Versailles to truly get the full experience that the palace has to offer.

who lived there and built and designed it, see pictures of its famous rooms, and even go on a 3D video tour of the buildings and grounds. You can also read other books about Versailles to learn more about this beautiful palace and its place in French history. Check out the "For More Information" section in the back of this book for the official web site address.

Regardless of how you visit Versailles, don't miss out on the opportunity to do so. It's truly one of the wonders of Europe and a place you'll want to explore, either in person or as an arm-chair traveler with a good book.

A FAMOUS VISITOR

Wolfgang Amadeus Mozart

In December 1763, during King Louis XV's reign, a young child prodigy—or musical genius—came to visit the royal family at the Palace of Versailles from Austria. His name was Wolfgang Amadeus Mozart. He was only six years old at the time. Mozart came with his father, mother, and older sister who was also a musician.

Mozart played for the King several times during the month his family spent in France. In early January 1764, the entire Mozart family was invited to eat at the king's table one evening. At this dinner, Mozart sat next to the queen. Following the meal, the king asked Mozart to play the organ in the royal chapel.

The Mozarts and the royal family made their way to the chapel. Mozart sat at the organ and started to play. The king was delighted with the beautiful music that filled the hall. Following this impromptu recital, the Mozart family was invited to stay at Versailles (instead of the hotel where they had been lodging) for another 16 days. Mozart continued to play for the royal family each day of his family's stay.[3]

1624 to 1631	Louis XIII builds a hunting lodge in the forests surrounding the village of Versailles.
May 14, 1643	Louis XIII dies and thereby his son, Louis XIV, the "Sun King," takes the throne.
1664 to 1668	First phase of construction occurs on the new palace at Versailles.
May 1664	Pleasures of the Enchanted Island is held at Versailles.
1666	Fountains play for the first time at Versailles.
1669 to 1672	Second phase of construction occurs at Versailles; Palace is enlarged.
1670	Mansart becomes head architect at Versailles. Interior decoration begins.
1674	Louis XIV resides at Versailles for the first time.
1677	Louis XIV decides that Versailles will be government seat of France.
1678 to 1684	Third phase of construction occurs at Versailles. Palace takes on the look we are familiar with today.
1682	Versailles officially becomes the capital of France. Courtiers and other officials take residence at the palace.
1683	Maria Theresa, wife of Louis XIV, dies.
1684	Hall of Mirrors is completed.
1688 to 1697	Fourth, and last, phase of construction at Versailles.
1714	King Louis XIV invites ambassador of Siam to a royal function at Versailles.
1715	Louis XIV dies after a 72-year reign. His great-grandson, Louis XV, is crowned king of France at age 5. The government seat is moved to Paris.
1717	Peter the Great, Tsar of Russia, visits Versailles.
1722	Louis XV returns the government seat, and his official residence, to Versailles.
1733	France becomes involved in the War of Polish Succession.
1735	Louis XV's favorite hot chocolate recipe is published in a French cookbook.
1740	France becomes involved in the War of Austrian Succession.
1756	France becomes involved in the Seven Years War.
December 1763	Mozart visits the royal court at Versailles.
1770	The future king Louis XVI marries Austrian princess Marie-Antoinette.
1774	Louis XV dies of small pox. Louis XVI becomes king at the age of 20.
March 20, 1778	Benjamin Franklin and other American delegates come to Versailles asking for French support for the American Revolution. Louis XVI agrees to the alliance.
1780	Marie-Antoinette builds a lavish theater in the Petit Trianon at Versailles.

1783	Marie-Antoinette builds her hamlet in the Petit Trianon. First hot air balloon ride in the world occurs at Versailles. Treaty of Paris, which officially ended the American Revolutionary War, is signed here at Versailles on September 3.
1788	It takes more than 88 percent of a commoner's wage to buy a loaf of bread.
October 1, 1789	Another lavish feast is held at Versailles for 210 guests.
October 6, 1789	An angry mob attacks Versailles and the royal family agree to go with them as prisoners. Louis XVI and Marie-Antoinette would never return to Versailles again.
1793	Louis XVI and Marie-Antoinette are both executed at the guillotine.
1833	Palace of Versailles is turned into a museum owned by the French people.
1855	Victoria, queen of England, visits Versailles.
1875	France's Third Republic is officially proclaimed at Versailles.
1896	Nicolas II, Tsar of Russia, visits Versailles.
June 28, 1919	Treaty of Versailles, which officially ends World War I, is signed in the Hall of Mirrors.
1920s	American billionaire John D. Rockefeller pays to have the palace's roof and other buildings at Versailles restored.
1938	George VI, king of England, visits Versailles.
1**952 to 1980**	Palace goes through a major restoration and conservation era.
1957	Elizabeth II, Queen of England, visits France for the first time as queen.
May 26, 1961	President John F. Kennedy and First Lady Jacqueline Kennedy attend a lavish state dinner in the Hall of Mirrors hosted by Charles de Gaulle.
1962-1966	Extensive renovations on the palace, especially the Grand Trianon. The Trianon-sous-Bois wing is converted into a Presidential residence used first by Charles de Gualle.
1999	Jacques Chirac, president of France, reopens the Trianon-sous-Bois to the public. An historic storm strikes France in December severely damaging the estate of Versailles: broken windows, damaged roofs, and more than 200,000 trees toppled, snapped, and uprooted. Many of the trees were rare species planted hundreds of years ago.
2000	Work on restoration of the gardens at Versailles (after the 1999 storm) begins.
2009	The Trianon-sous-Bois is returned to the public and is managed by the Versailles estate.
2014	Versailles is considered a top tourist attraction in the world with millions of people coming to tour the palace and gardens every year.

Introduction: A Famous Alliance at Versailles

1. Walter Isaacson, *Benjamin Franklin, An American Life* (New York: Simon & Schuster, 2003), p 348.

Chapter 1

1. Francis Loring Payne, *The Story of Versailles* (New York: Moffat, Yard & Company, 1919) http://www.gutenberg.org/files/14857/14857-h/14857-h.htm.
2. Ibid.
3. "André Le Nôtre," *Chateau De Versailles,* http://en.chateauversailles.fr/history-/versailles-during-the-centuries/the-palace-construction/andre-le-notre-
1613-1700
4. J.H. Shennan, *Louis XIV* (London: Metheun & Co. Ltd., 1986), p.9
5. "The Pleasures of the Enchanted Island," Chateau De Versailles,
http://en.chateauversailles.fr/history/versailles-during-the-centuries/living-at-the-court/festivities-les-plaisirs-de-lile-enchantee-the-pleasures-
6. Payne.
7. Marie Antoinette and the French Revolution, "Entrance," PBS.org,
http://www.pbs.org/marieantoinette/life/index.html?utm_source=
Tumblr&utm_medium=ThisDayHistory&utm_campaign=August%2B23%2BLouis%2BXVI
8. Marie Antoinette and the French Revolution, "Hall of Mirrors," PBS.org,
http://www.pbs.org/marieantoinette/life/mirrors.html

Chapter 2

1. "Modern History Sourcebook: Duc de Saint-Simon: The Court of Louis XIV" http://www.fordham.edu/halsall/mod/17stsimon.asp
2. "A Day in the Life of Louis XIV," Chateau De Versailles,
http://en.chateauversailles.fr/history/versailles-during-the-centuries/living-at-the-court/a-day-in-the-life-of-louis-xiv
3. "Royal Tables," Chateau De Versailles,
http://en.chateauversailles.fr/history/versailles-during-the-centuries/living-at-the-court/royal-tables-
4. Payne.
5. "The Pleasures of the Enchanted Island," Chateau De Versailles,
http://en.chateauversailles.fr/history/versailles-during-the-centuries/living-at-the-court/festivities-les-plaisirs-de-lile-enchantee-the-pleasures-
6. Payne.

Chapter 3

1. "King Louis XV," Biography.com,
http://www.biography.com/people/louis-xv-9386921
2. "1722 Retour of the Court to Versailles," Chateau De Versailles,
http://en.chateauversailles.fr/history/the-great-days/most-important-dates/1722-retour-of-the-court-to-versailles
3. Richard Covington, "Renaissance of the Gardens of Versailles," Smithsonian. July 2001, p.90.
4. "Chocolate at Versailles," Chateau De Versailles,
http://en.chateauversailles.fr/index.php?option=com_cdvfiche&idf=B3C55317-3653-AF05-CF4C-AF7C8BBA9DF0

Chapter 4

1. Marie Antoinette and the French Revolution, "Entrance," PBS.org, http://www.pbs.org/marieantoinette/life/index.html?utm_source=Tumblr&utm_medium=ThisDayHistory&utm_campaign=August%2B23%2BLouis%2BXVI
2. "The Queen's Hamlet," Chateau De Versailles, http://en.chateauversailles.fr/discover-the-estate/le-domaine-de-marie-antoinette/the-queen-hamlet/the-queens-hamlet
3. "The First Aerostatic Flight," Chateau De Versailles, http://en.chateauversailles.fr/history/versailles-during-the-centuries/living-at-the-court/the-first-aerostatic-flight

Chapter 5

1. Lisa Bramen, "When Food Changed History: The French Revolution," Smithsonian.com, July 24, 2010, http://www.smithsonianmag.com/arts-culture/when-food-changed-history-the-french-revolution-93598442/?no-ist
2. "World's Most Visited Tourist Attractions, No. 39, Palace of Versailles, Versailles, France," TravelandLeisure.com, http://www.travelandleisure.com/articles/worlds-most-visited-tourist-attractions/40
3. "1763-1764 Visit of the child Mozart," Chateau De Versailles, http://en.chateauversailles.fr/history/the-significant-dates/chronology/1763-1764-visit-of-the-child-mozart/1763-visit-of-the-child-m/december-1763---january-1764-1

Further Reading

Books

Blohm, Craig E. *The Palace of Versailles (History's Great Structures).* San Diego, CA: ReferencePoint Press, 2014.

Heinrich, Christian. *The Palace of Versailles.* Okon, UK: Moonlight Publishing, 2012.

Lasky, Kathryn. *The Royal Diaries: Marie Antoinette, Princess of Versailles, Austria-France, 1769.* New York: Scholastic, Inc., 2013.

Priceman, Majorie. *Hot Air: The (Mostly) True Story of the First Hot-Air Balloon Ride.* New York: Athenaeum Books for Young Readers, 2005.

Steves, Rick. *Rick Steves' Tour: Versailles.* Berkeley, CA: Avalon Travel Publishing, 2012.

Works Consulted

"1722 Retour of the Court to Versailles," Chateau De Versailles, http://en.chateauversailles.fr/history/the-great-days/most-important-dates/1722-retour-of-the-court-to-versailles

"1763-1764 Visit of the child Mozart," Chateau De Versailles, http://en.chateauversailles.fr/history/the-significant-dates/chronology/1763-1764-visit-of-the-child-mozart/1763-visit-of-the-child-m/december-1763---january-1764-1

"André Le Nôtre," Chateau De Versailles, http://en.chateauversailles.fr/history-/versailles-during-the-centuries/the-palace-construction/andre-le-notre-1613-1700

"A Day in the Life of Louis XIV," Chateau De Versailles, http://en.chateauversailles.fr/history/versailles-during-the-centuries/living-at-the-court/a-day-in-the-life-of-louis-xiv

Bramen, Lisa. "When Food Changed History: The French Revolution," Smithsonian.com, July 24, 2010, http://www.smithsonianmag.com/arts-culture/when-food-changed-history-the-french-revolution-93598442/?no-ist

Covington, Richard. "Renaissance of the Gardens of Versailles," *Smithsonian.* July 2001, p.90."Chocolate at Versailles," Chateau De Versailles, http://en.chateau

"First Aerostatic Flight," Chateau De Versailles, http://en.chateauversailles.fr/history/versailles-during-the-centuries/living-at-the-court/the-first-aerostatic-flight

Isaacson, Walter. *Benjamin Franklin, An American Life.* New York: Simon & Schuster, 2003.

Jarus, Owen. "Palace of Versailles: Facts and History," LiveScience.com. August 14, 2013. http://www.livescience.com/38903-palace-of-versailles-facts-history.html

"King Louis XV," Biography.com, http://www.biography.com/people/louis-xv-9386921

Marie Antoinette and the French Revolution, "Entrance," PBS.org, http://www.pbs.org/marieantoinette/life/index.html?utm_source=Tumblr&utm_medium=ThisDayHistory&utm_campaign=August%2B23%2BLouis%2BXVI

Marie Antoinette and the French Revolution, "Hall of Mirrors," PBS.org, http://www.pbs.org/marieantoinette/life/mirrors.html

"Modern History Sourcebook: Duc de Saint-Simon: The Court of Louis XIV" http://www.fordham.edu/halsall/mod/17stsimon.asp

Payne, Francis Loring. *The Story of Versailles.* New York: Moffat, Yard & Company, 1919. http://www.gutenberg.org/files/14857/14857-h/14857-h.htm.

"Pleasures of the Enchanted Island," Chateau De Versailles, http://en.chateauversailles.fr/history/versailles-during-the-centuries/living-at-the-court/festivities-les-plaisirs-de-lile-enchantee-the-pleasures-

"Royal Tables," Chateau De Versailles, http://en.chateauversailles.fr/history/versailles-during-the-centuries/living-at-the-court/royal-tables-

Shennan, J.H. *Louis XIV.* London: Metheun & Co. Ltd., 1986.versailles.fr/index.php?option=com_cdvfiche&idf=B3C55317-3653-AF05-CF4C-AF7C8BBA9DF0

"The Queen's Hamlet," Chateau De Versailles, http://en.chateauversailles.fr/discover-the-estate/le-domaine-de-marie-antoinette/the-queen-hamlet/the-queens-hamlet

"World's Most Visited Tourist Attractions, No. 39, Palace of Versailles, Versailles, France," TravelandLeisure.com, http://www.travelandleisure.com/articles/worlds-most-visited-tourist-attractions/40

On the Internet

Office of Tourism, Versailles
http://www.versailles-tourisme.com/en/accueil.html

Palace of Versailles
http://en.chateauversailles.fr/

Palace and Park of Versailles
http://whc.unesco.org/en/list/83

Travel for Kids, Versailles
http://www.travelforkids.com/Funtodo/France/versailles.htm

Glossary

aerostatic (air-OH-stah-tic)—An aircraft like a balloon or dirigible.

alliance (uh-LIE-uhns)—A close association of nations or groups.

architect (AR-kih-tehkt)—A professional who designs or supervises the construction of buildings.

aristocrat (uh-RIH-stow-crat)—A member of a ruling class or nobility.

Bastille (BAA-still)—A fortress in Paris used as a prison or jail.

bedchamber (bed-CHAYM-ber)—A bedroom.

conservatory (Kuhn-SERV-uh-toree)—A greenhouse where plants are grown.

couchee (koo-jee)—The process or ceremony of going to bed, especially for royalty.

court (kort)—A group of people who attend to or advise the king or queen.

gondola (gahn-DOH-luh)—A flat-bottomed rowing boat.

legacy (leh-GUH-see)—A reputation received from an ancestor.

levee (LEH-vee)—The act of rising in the morning.

opulent (AH-pew-luhnt)—Very fancy or exquisite.

orangerie (ORANGE-er-ee)—A place where orange trees grow.

porter (POR-ter)—A doorkeeper.

saplings (SAAP-lings)—Small trees that have just started to grow.

smallpox (SMALL-pocks)—A disease that causes sores across the skin.

Index